Please Sign

GUEST BOOK

Even though you're growing up, you should

NEVER STOP HAVING FUN.

NINA DOBREV

Guests

A message...

Guests

_____

_____

_____

_____

A message...

_____

_____

_____

_____

Guests

_____

_____

_____

_____

A message...

_____

_____

_____

_____

Guests

_____

_____

_____

_____

A message...

_____

_____

_____

_____

Guests

_____

_____

_____

_____

A message...

_____

_____

_____

_____

Guests

_____

_____

_____

_____

A message...

_____

_____

_____

_____

Guests

A message...

Guests

_____

_____

_____

_____

A message...

_____

_____

_____

_____

Guests

_____

_____

_____

_____

A message...

_____

_____

_____

_____

Guests

_____

_____

_____

_____

A message...

_____

_____

_____

_____

Guests

_____

_____

_____

_____

A message...

_____

_____

_____

_____

Guests

A message...

Guests

_____

_____

_____

_____

A message...

_____

_____

_____

_____

Guests

_____

_____

_____

_____

A message...

_____

_____

_____

_____

Guests

_____

_____

_____

_____

A message...

_____

_____

_____

_____

Guests

_____

_____

_____

_____

A message...

_____

_____

_____

_____

Guests

_____

_____

_____

_____

A message...

_____

_____

_____

_____

Guests

_____

_____

_____

_____

A message...

_____

_____

_____

_____

Guests

A message...

Guests

_____

_____

_____

_____

A message...

_____

_____

_____

_____

Guests

_____

_____

_____

_____

A message...

_____

_____

_____

_____

Guests

_____

_____

_____

_____

A message...

_____

_____

_____

_____

Guests

A message...

Guests

_____

_____

_____

_____

A message...

_____

_____

_____

_____

Guests

_____

_____

_____

_____

A message...

_____

_____

_____

_____

Guests

A message...

Guests

_____

_____

_____

_____

A message...

_____

_____

_____

_____

Guests

_____

_____

_____

_____

A message...

_____

_____

_____

_____

Guests

_____

_____

_____

_____

A message...

_____

_____

_____

_____

Guests

A message...

Guests

_____

_____

_____

_____

A message...

_____

_____

_____

_____

Guests

_____

_____

_____

_____

A message...

_____

_____

_____

_____

Guests

_____

_____

_____

_____

A message...

_____

_____

_____

_____

Guests

_____

_____

_____

_____

A message...

_____

_____

_____

_____

Guests

_____

_____

_____

_____

A message...

_____

_____

_____

_____

Guests

_____

_____

_____

_____

A message...

_____

_____

_____

_____

Guests

_____

_____

_____

_____

A message...

_____

_____

_____

_____

Guests

_____

_____

_____

_____

A message...

_____

_____

_____

_____

Guests

_____

_____

_____

_____

A message...

_____

_____

_____

_____

Guests

A message...

Guests

_____

_____

_____

_____

A message...

_____

_____

_____

_____

Guests

_____

_____

_____

_____

A message...

_____

_____

_____

_____

Guests

_____

_____

_____

_____

A message...

_____

_____

_____

_____

Guests

_____

_____

_____

_____

A message...

_____

_____

_____

_____

Guests

_____

_____

_____

_____

A message...

_____

_____

_____

_____

Guests

_____

_____

_____

_____

A message...

_____

_____

_____

_____

Guests

_____

_____

_____

_____

A message...

_____

_____

_____

_____

Guests

_____

_____

_____

_____

A message...

_____

_____

_____

_____

Guests

_____

_____

_____

_____

A message...

_____

_____

_____

_____

Guests

_____

_____

_____

_____

A message...

_____

_____

_____

_____

Guests

A message...

Guests

_____

_____

_____

_____

A message...

_____

_____

_____

_____

Guests

_____

_____

_____

_____

A message...

_____

_____

_____

_____

Guests

_____

_____

_____

_____

A message...

_____

_____

_____

_____

Guests

_____

_____

_____

_____

A message...

_____

_____

_____

_____

Guests

_____

_____

_____

A message...

_____

_____

_____

Guests

A message...

Guests

_____

_____

_____

_____

A message...

_____

_____

_____

_____

Guests

_____

_____

_____

_____

A message...

_____

_____

_____

_____

Guests

_____

_____

_____

_____

A message...

_____

_____

_____

_____

Guests

_____

_____

_____

_____

A message...

_____

_____

_____

_____

Guests

_____

_____

_____

_____

A message...

_____

_____

_____

_____

Guests

_____

_____

_____

_____

A message...

_____

_____

_____

_____

Guests

A message...

Guests

_____

_____

_____

_____

A message...

_____

_____

_____

_____

Guests

_____

_____

_____

_____

A message...

_____

_____

_____

_____

Guests

_____

_____

_____

_____

A message...

_____

_____

_____

_____

Guests

_____

_____

_____

_____

A message...

_____

_____

_____

_____

Guests

_____

_____

_____

_____

A message...

_____

_____

_____

Guests

_____

_____

_____

_____

A message...

_____

_____

_____

_____

Guests

_____

_____

_____

_____

A message...

_____

_____

_____

_____

Guests

A message...

Guests

A message...

Guests

A message...

Guests

_____

_____

_____

_____

A message...

_____

_____

_____

_____

Guests

_____

_____

_____

_____

A message...

_____

_____

_____

_____

Guests

_____

_____

_____

_____

A message...

_____

_____

_____

_____

Guests

A message...

Guests

_____

_____

_____

_____

A message...

_____

_____

_____

_____

Guests

_____

_____

_____

_____

A message...

_____

_____

_____

_____

Guests

_____

_____

_____

_____

A message...

_____

_____

_____

_____

Guests

_____

_____

_____

_____

A message...

_____

_____

_____

_____

Guests

_____

_____

_____

_____

A message...

_____

_____

_____

_____

Guests

A message...

Guests

_____

_____

_____

_____

A message...

_____

_____

_____

Guests

_____

_____

_____

_____

A message...

_____

_____

_____

_____

Guests

A message...

Guests

A message...

Guests

_____

_____

_____

_____

A message...

_____

_____

_____

_____

Guests

A message...

Guests

_____

_____

_____

_____

A message...

_____

_____

_____

_____

Guests

A message...

Guests

A message...

Guests

_____

_____

_____

_____

A message...

_____

_____

_____

_____

Guests

_____

_____

_____

_____

A message...

_____

_____

_____

_____

Guests

A message...

Guests

_____

_____

_____

_____

A message...

_____

_____

_____

_____

Guests

_____

_____

_____

_____

A message...

_____

_____

_____

_____

Guests

_____

_____

_____

_____

A message...

_____

_____

_____

_____

Guests

A message...

Guests

A message...

Guests

_____

_____

_____

_____

A message...

_____

_____

_____

_____

Guests

_____

_____

_____

_____

A message...

_____

_____

_____

_____

Guests

A message...

Guests

_____

_____

_____

_____

A message...

_____

_____

_____

Guests

_____

_____

_____

_____

A message...

_____

_____

_____

_____

Guests

_____

_____

_____

_____

A message...

_____

_____

_____

_____

Guests

A message...

Guests

_____

_____

_____

_____

A message...

_____

_____

_____

_____

Guests

_____

_____

_____

_____

A message...

_____

_____

_____

_____

Guests

A message...

_____

_____

_____

_____

_____

_____

_____

Guests

A message...

Guests

_____

_____

_____

_____

A message...

_____

_____

_____

Guests

_____

_____

_____

_____

A message...

_____

_____

_____

_____

Guests

A message...

GUEST

GIFT

GUEST   GIFT

_____   _____

_____   _____

_____   _____

_____   _____

_____   _____

_____   _____

_____   _____

_____   _____

_____   _____

_____   _____

Gifts

GUEST   GIFT

_____   _____
_____   _____
_____   _____
_____   _____
_____   _____
_____   _____
_____   _____
_____   _____
_____   _____
_____   _____

GUEST   GIFT

_____ _____

_____ _____

_____ _____

_____ _____

_____ _____

_____ _____

_____ _____

_____ _____

_____ _____

_____ _____

Gifts

GUEST	GIFT

Gifts

GUEST   GIFT

_____   _____

_____   _____

_____   _____

_____   _____

_____   _____

_____   _____

_____   _____

_____   _____

_____   _____

_____   _____

Gifts

GUEST	GIFT

GUEST

GIFT

Made in United States
North Haven, CT
13 May 2023

36542486R00072